For Meir and Dovid,
Our little rovers who like to roam
And for Nomi,
Our home base —R.H.

For Jackson —K.R.

Published by Roaring Brook Press
Roaring Brook Press is a division of
Holtzbrinck Publishing Holdings Limited Partnership
120 Broadway, New York, NY 10271
mackids.com

Library of Congress Control Number: 2019932581
ISBN: 978-1-250-19833-4

Our books may be purchased in bulk for promotional, educational, or business use.
Please contact your local bookseller or the Macmillan Corporate and Premium Sales Department
at (800) 221-7945 ext. 5442 or by email at MacmillanSpecialMarkets@macmillan.com.

First edition, 2019
Book design by Andrew Arnold
Printed in China by RR Donnelley Asia Printing Solutions Ltd., Dongguan City, Guangdong Province

10 9 8 7 6 5 4 3 2 1

RED ROVER

CURIOSITY ON MARS

Written by

RICHARD HO

Illustrated by

KATHERINE ROY

ROARING BROOK PRESS
New York

The little rover likes to roam.
It leaves long, straight tracks as it goes.

The tracks play hide-and-seek . . .

. . . waiting for the rover to find them again.

The rover never gets tired.
It crosses plains,
climbs hills,

and traces the
bottoms of craters.

It rolls on and on.

It is curious.
It wants to learn about
the world around it.

ZAP!

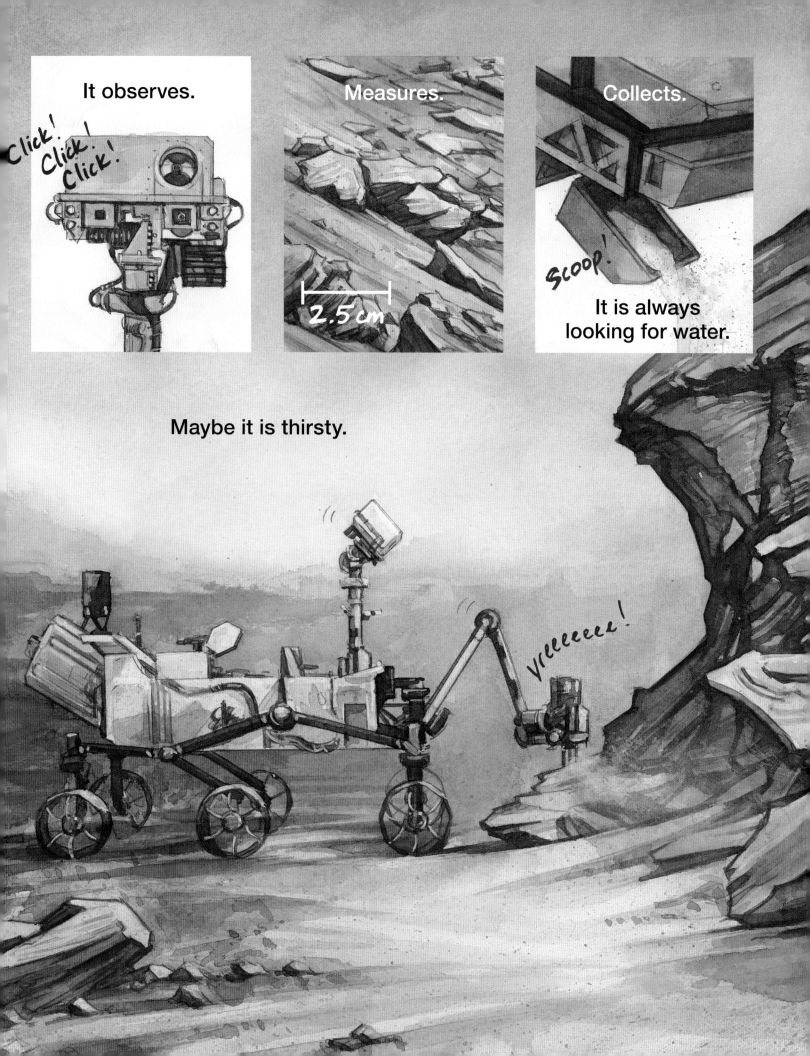

The rover seems lonely, roaming by itself.
But it is not alone.
It has friends that came before.

and journeyed
far and wide.

They had a spirit
of adventure

and seized every
opportunity to explore.

Sojourner

Spirit

Opportunity

Just like this rover.
Like them, it looks up.

It talks to whoever sent it.
It tells them what it is like here.

Barren . . .
but not lifeless.

ZAP!

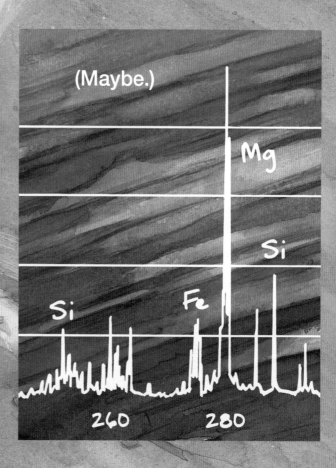

(Maybe.)

It is not easy to live here.

You might get stuck in the sand.

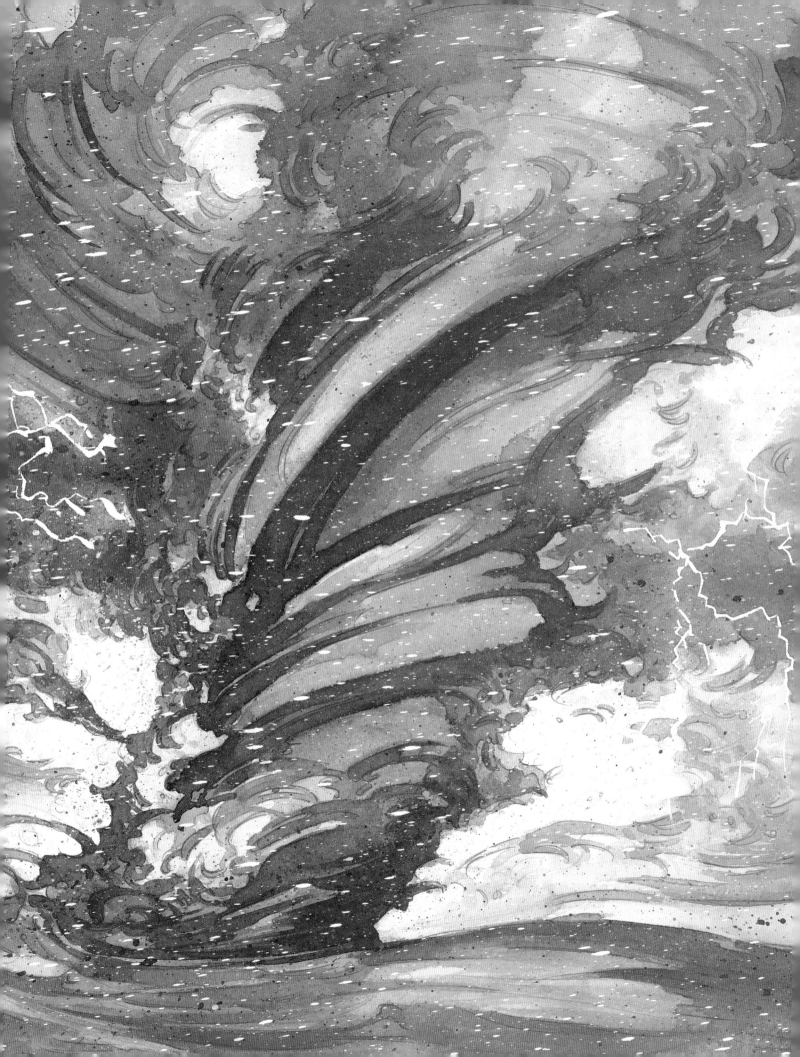

Everything is . . .

as far as the eye can see.
But it is beautiful.

They call me Mars.

I am not like your world.

I am cold.
I am every shade of red.
I am very far away.

But I am not alone.
I see the rover. I see its friends.

I see the stars, and I wonder . . .

. . . who will visit next?

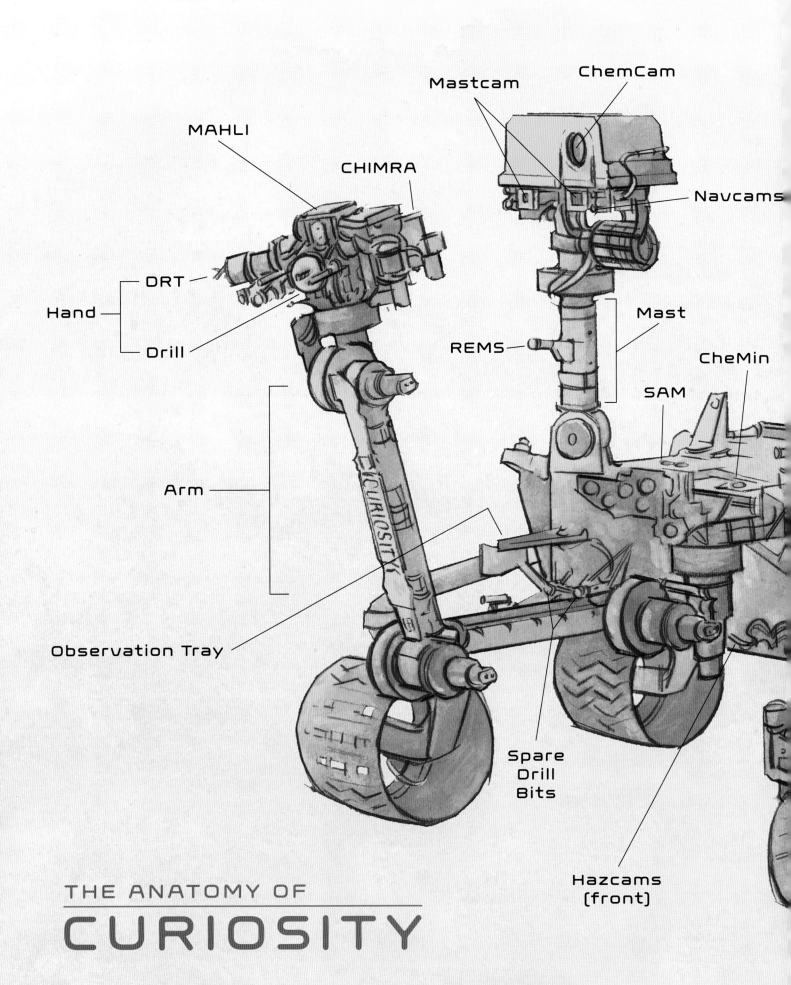

MAHLI

CHIMRA

Mastcam

ChemCam

Navcams

Hand
DRT
Drill

REMS

Mast

CheMin

SAM

Arm

Observation Tray

Spare Drill Bits

Hazcams (front)

THE ANATOMY OF
CURIOSITY

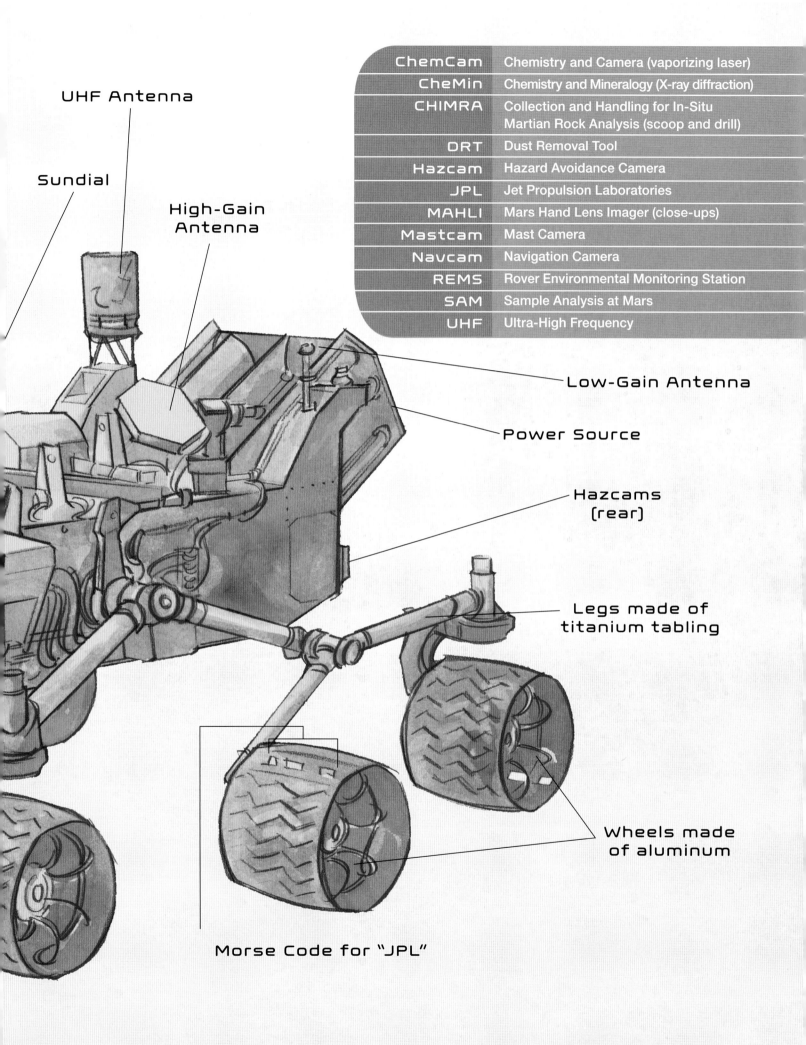

UHF Antenna

Sundial

High-Gain
Antenna

ChemCam	Chemistry and Camera (vaporizing laser)
CheMin	Chemistry and Mineralogy (X-ray diffraction)
CHIMRA	Collection and Handling for In-Situ Martian Rock Analysis (scoop and drill)
DRT	Dust Removal Tool
Hazcam	Hazard Avoidance Camera
JPL	Jet Propulsion Laboratories
MAHLI	Mars Hand Lens Imager (close-ups)
Mastcam	Mast Camera
Navcam	Navigation Camera
REMS	Rover Environmental Monitoring Station
SAM	Sample Analysis at Mars
UHF	Ultra-High Frequency

Low-Gain Antenna

Power Source

Hazcams
(rear)

Legs made of
titanium tabling

Wheels made
of aluminum

Morse Code for "JPL"

CURIOSITY BECAME THE DRIVING FORCE

of Mars exploration on August 6, 2012. That's when the rover touched down in Gale Crater after a nine-month journey from Earth. The fourth NASA rover to land successfully on the Red Planet, *Curiosity* is also the biggest and most advanced. Nearly ten feet long and weighing two thousand pounds, the car-sized laboratory is equipped with many scientific instruments, including a robotic arm, infrared laser, and seventeen cameras. If one of those cameras spots an interesting rock, *Curiosity* can vaporize a tiny piece with its laser and then analyze the chemical signature. The rover can also swing its arm over for a closer look with a microscope, or drill into the rock and bring a sample aboard for further scanning.

These tools help *Curiosity* carry out its main mission: studying the geology and climate of Mars to determine whether the planet had the necessary ingredients (including water) to support life in the past. Based on its discoveries so far, the answer is yes! Carbon dioxide, oxygen, hydrogen, and even water itself have all been detected in Martian rocks. *Curiosity* has uncovered evidence of ancient streambeds carved by flowing water, as well as layers of rocks at the bottom of long-disappeared lakes that contain chemical elements necessary for microscopic life.

In seven years of exploration, *Curiosity* has traveled over twelve miles and made countless invaluable observations along the way. It has snapped some of the most detailed photographs of Mars (including some selfies) and dug deeper into the layers of history beneath its wheels than any rover before. And it's still rolling to this day!

Of course, the success of *Curiosity* was made possible by the friends that paved the way . . .

— CURIOSITY'S FRIENDS —

MARINER 9
TYPE: Orbiter
LAUNCHED: May 30, 1971
ARRIVED: November 14, 1971

Part of a series of probes sent by NASA to study the inner planets, *Mariner 9* was the fourth to successfully reach Mars. The first spacecraft to orbit another planet, it spent almost a year mapping the surface and studying the atmosphere before it was deactivated. NASA predicts it will remain in orbit until 2022, when it is expected to burn up in the atmosphere or crash into the planet's surface.

VIKING 1
TYPE: Lander
LAUNCHED: August 20, 1975
LANDED: July 20, 1976

One of two identical spacecraft sent to land on Mars, *Viking 1* was the first to accomplish the feat! (*Viking 2* followed just two months later.) *Viking 1* took the first color photographs of the Martian surface and conducted experiments for more than six years before it lost contact with NASA.

PATHFINDER AND SOJOURNER
TYPE: Lander and Rover
LAUNCHED: December 4, 1996
LANDED: July 4, 1997

Unlike previous landers, *Pathfinder* brought a partner: *Sojourner*! The first Mars rover was also the smallest, measuring just two feet long and weighing twenty-three pounds. Using *Pathfinder* as a home base, *Sojourner* roamed free and captured over five hundred pictures of the surrounding landscape. It also conducted experiments on Martian rocks, soil, and wind. By the time *Pathfinder* lost contact with Earth, *Sojourner* had driven for almost three months and traveled just over 330 feet.

SPIRIT AND OPPORTUNITY

TYPE: Rovers

LAUNCHED: June 10, 2003 (Spirit), July 7, 2003 (Opportunity)

LANDED: January 4, 2004 (Spirit), January 25, 2004 (Opportunity)

These twin rovers arrived just three weeks apart, but on opposite sides of the planet. Both *Spirit* and *Opportunity* were tasked with studying rocks and soil for clues of past water activity on Mars. Within the first two months, *Opportunity* discovered rock layers that were likely created by a large body of water. This was the first evidence that liquid water once flowed on the surface of Mars! Both rovers made many important observations of Martian geology and weather, including dust storms that cover large parts of the planet. Unfortunately, *Spirit* got stuck in a pit of soft soil in 2009. NASA tried unsuccessfully to free the rover, and finally lost contact in 2010. *Opportunity* kept exploring, and by 2018 had traveled twenty-eight miles—the longest distance driven outside Earth! But during the summer of 2018, a massive global dust storm forced the rover into hibernation. NASA lost contact on June 10, 2018, and, after an additional six months of trying to contact the rover, officially declared the end of *Opportunity*'s mission on February 13, 2019. The fifteen-year mission makes *Opportunity* the longest lasting robot on the surface of another planet.

MARS 2020 ROVER

EXPECTED LAUNCH: July—August 2020

EXPECTED LANDING: February 2021

Curiosity will soon have another friend! NASA plans to send a new rover to Mars in 2020. Based on *Curiosity*'s design, the still-unnamed rover will carry a different set of tools and instruments—including a small helicopter! The rover will land in a region likely to have been habitable in the past. There, it will search for signs of past life and study current environmental conditions to help NASA plan future manned missions to Mars. In another first, the rover will also collect rock and soil samples and leave them in sealed tubes on the planet's surface. That will make it easier for future missions to collect the samples and bring them back to Earth for further study!

MARS AT A GLANCE

- Fourth planet from the Sun
- Italian scientist Galileo Galilei was the first to observe it through a telescope
- About half the diameter of Earth
- Gravity is about one-third as strong as Earth's
- Atmosphere is about 1 percent as dense as Earth's
- Average surface temperature is -81 degrees Fahrenheit
- Reddish color comes from iron oxide dust (rust) on the surface and in the atmosphere, though drilling sometimes reveals that the rock below the surface is blue
- Dust devils, swirling funnels of wind and dust, can reach up to twelve miles high
- Largest dust storms in the solar system; some can cover nearly the entire planet
- Maximum wind speeds of sixty miles per hour
- Lightning has been detected in Martian dust storms, but the atmosphere is probably too thin to carry the sound of thunder very far
- Frozen water is locked in the polar ice caps, though liquid water might exist on certain steep slopes and in an underground lake
- Home to Olympus Mons, the tallest volcano in the solar system
- Two small moons, Phobos and Deimos

BIBLIOGRAPHY

> Carney, Elizabeth. *National Geographic Readers: Mars*. Des Moines, IA: National Geographic Children's Books, 2014.
> Hamilton, John. *Curiosity Rover: Searching for Life on Mars*. Minneapolis, MN: A&D Xtreme, 2017. Xtreme Spacecraft Series.
> "Mars Science Laboratory Curiosity Rover." Jet Propulsion Laboratory, California Institute of Technology. mars.nasa.gov/msl.
> "Mission to Mars: Mars Science Laboratory Curiosity Rover." Jet Propulsion Laboratory, California Institute of Technology. jpl.nasa.gov/missions/mars-science-laboratory-curiosity-rover-msl.
> Kaufman, Marc. *Mars Up Close: Inside the Curiosity Mission*. Des Moines, IA: National Geographic, 2014.
> Manning, Rob, and William L. Simon. *Mars Rover Curiosity: An Inside Account from Curiosity's Chief Engineer*. Washington, DC: Smithsonian Books, 2014.
> Rusch, Elizabeth. *The Mighty Mars Rovers: The Incredible Adventures of Spirit and Opportunity*. Scientists in the Field Series. Boston, MA: Houghton Mifflin Books for Children, 2012.
> Siy, Alexandra. *Cars on Mars: Roving the Red Planet*. Reprint ed., Watertown, MA: Charlesbridge, 2011.

WEBSITES

NASA: nasa.gov
Jet Propulsion Laboratory: jpl.nasa.gov

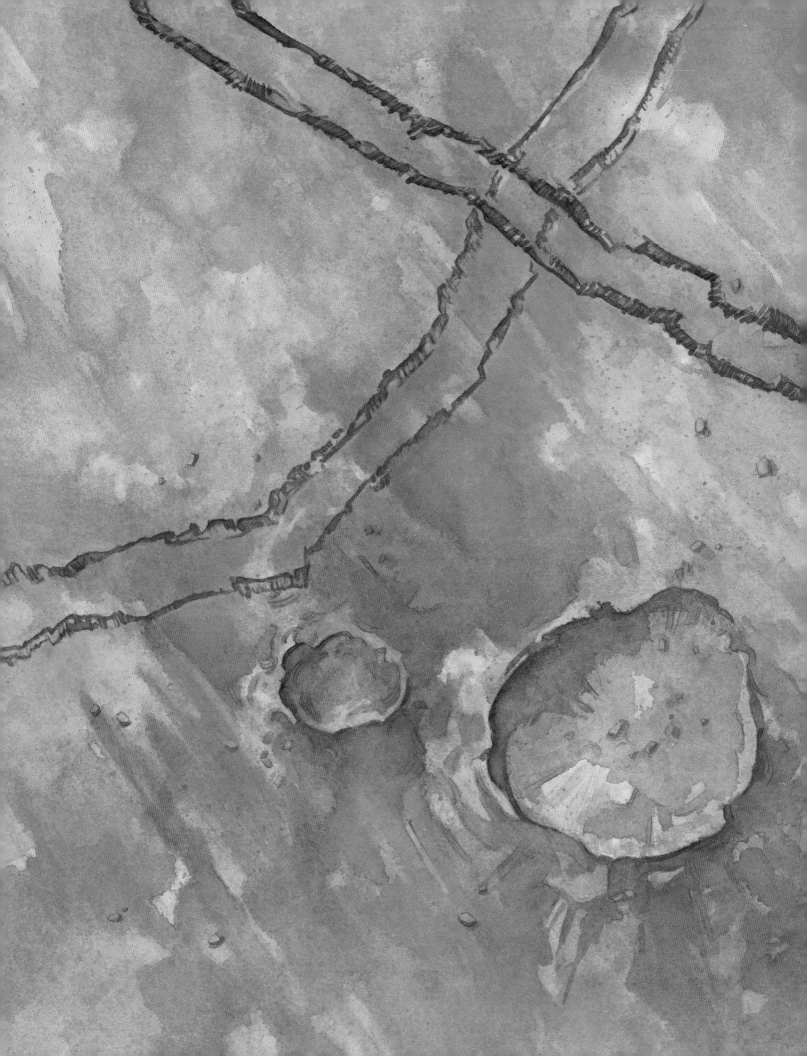